The City in Which I Love You is the 1990 Lamont Poetry Selection of The Academy of American Poets.

From 1954 through 1974 the Lamont Poetry Selection supported the publication and distribution of a first collection of poems. Since 1975 this distinguished award has been given for an American poet's second book.

Judges for 1990: *Marvin Bell, Sandra McPherson, and Robert Morgan.*

The City in Which I Love You

The City in Which I Love You

Poems by *Li-Young Lee*

BOA Editions, Ltd. / Brockport, New York / 1990

ISBN: 0-918526-82-5 Cloth
ISBN: 0-918526-83-3 Paper

LC #: 90-61416

Publications by BOA Editions, Ltd.
are made possible with the assistance of grants from the Literature Program of the New York State Council on the Arts and the Literature Program of the National Endowment for the Arts, as well as with financial assistance from private foundations, corporations and individuals.

BOA Editions, Ltd. is a non-profit literary organization.

Cover Image: "Map of Rome," Illumination from
Très Riches Heures de Jean, duc de Berry
Courtesy of Musée Condé, Chateau de Chantilly
Cover Design: Daphne Poulin
BOA Logo: Mirko

Typesetting: Visual Studies Workshop
Manufacturing: McNaughton & Gunn, Lithographers

10 9 8 7 6

BOA Editions, Ltd.
A. Poulin, Jr., President
92 Park Avenue
Brockport, NY 14420

Contents

for Donna, again

I

Furious Versions

1.

These days I waken in the used light
of someone's spent life, to discover
the birds have stripped my various names of meaning entire:
the sparrow by quarrel,
the dove by grievance.
I lie
dismantled. I feel
the hours. Do they veer
to dusk? Or dawn?
Will I rise and go
out into an American city?
Or walk down to the wilderness sea?
I might run with wife and children to the docks
to bribe an officer for our lives
and perilous passage.
Then I'd answer
in an oceanic tongue
to *Professor, Capitalist, Husband, Father.*
Or I might have one more
hour of sleep before my father
comes to take me
to his snowbound church
where I dust the pews and he sets candles
out the color of teeth.
That means I was born in Bandung, 1958;
on my father's back, in borrowed clothes,
I came to America.

And I wonder
if I imagined those wintry mornings
in a dim nave, since
I'm the only one
who's lived to tell it,
and I confuse
the details; was it my father's skin
which shone like teeth?
Was it his heart that lay snowbound?
But if I waken to a jailer
rousting me to meet my wife and son,
come to see me in my cell
where I eat the chocolate
and smoke the cigarettes they smuggle,
what name do I answer to?
And did I stand
on the train from Chicago to Pittsburgh
so my fevered son could sleep? Or did I
open my eyes
and see my father's closed face
rocking above me?

Memory revises me.
Even now a letter
comes from a place
I don't know, from someone
with my name
and postmarked years ago,
while I await
injunctions from the light
or the dark;
I wait for shapeliness
limned, or dissolution.
Is paradise due or narrowly missed
until another thousand years?

I wait
in a blue hour
and faraway noise of hammering,
and on a page a poem begun, something
about to be dispersed,
something about to come into being.

2.

I wake to black
and one sound—
neither a heart
approaching nor one shoe
coming, but something
less measured, never
arriving. I wander
a house I thought I knew;
I walk the halls as if the halls
of that other
mansion, my father's heart.
I follow the sound
past a black window
where a bird sits like a blacker
question, *To where? To where? To where?*
Past my mother's room where her
knees creak, *Meaning. Meaning.*
While a rose
rattles at my ear, *Where*
is your father?
And the silent house
booms, *Gone. Long gone.*

A door jumps
out from shadows,
then jumps away. This
is what I've come to find:
the back door, unlatched.
Tooled by an insular wind, it
slams and slams
without meaning
to and without meaning.

3.

Moonlight and high wind.
Dark poplars toss, insinuate the sea.
The yard heaves, perplexed
with shadows massed
and with shadows falling away.
Before me a tree, distinct
in its terrible
aspects, emerges, reels, sinks,
and is lost.
At my feet, shapes
tear free, separate darknesses
mingle, then crawl to the common
dark, lost.
At the brink
of my own now-here now-gone
shadow stand three flowers,
or two flowers,
and one's shade.
Impatiens? Alyssum?
Something forbids me to speak
of them in this
upheaval of forms and
voices—there are voices
now, plaintive, anxious.
I hear
interrogation in vague tongues.
I hear ocean sounds and a history of rain.
Somewhere a streetlamp,
and my brother never coming.
Somewhere a handful of hair and a lost box of letters.
And everywhere, fire,
corridors of fire, brick and barbed wire.

Soldiers sweep the streets
for my father. My mother
hides him, haggard,
in the closet.
The booted ones herd us
to the sea.
Waves furl, boats
and bodies drift out, farther out.
My father holds my hand, he says,
Don't forget any of this.
A short, bony-faced corporal
asks politely, deferring to class,
What color suit, Professor, would you like
to be buried in? Brown or blue?
A pistol butt turns my father's spit to blood.

It was a tropical night.
It was a half a year of sweat and fatal memory.
It was one year of fire
out of the world's diary of fires,
flesh-laced, mid-century fire,
teeth and hair infested,
napalm-dressed and skull-hung fire,
and imminent fire, an elected
fire come to rob me
of my own death, my damp bed
in the noisy earth,
my rocking toward a hymn-like night.

How, then, may I
speak of flowers
here, where
a world of forms convulses,

here, amidst
drafts—yet
these are not drafts
toward a future form, but
furious versions
of the here and now....

Here, now, one
should say nothing
of three flowers,
only enter with them
in silence, fear, and hope,
into the next nervous one hundred human years.

4.

But I see these flowers, and they seize
my mind, and I
can no more un-see
them than I can un-dream
this, no more than
the mind can stop
its wandering over the things
of the world, snagged on the world
as it is.
The mind is
a flowering
cut into time,
a rose,

the wandering rose
that scaled the red brick
of my father's house in Pennsylvania.
What was its name?
Each bloom, unsheathed
in my mind, urges, *Remember!*
The Paul's Scarlet!
Paul, who promised the coming
of the perfect and the departing of the imperfect,
Else why stand we in jeopardy every hour?

I thought of Paul
the morning I stepped out my door
and into an explosion of wings,
thudding and flapping, heavenly blows.

Blinded, I knew the day
of fierce judgement and rapture
had come. I thought
even the dooryard rose,
touched by wind, trembling
in anticipation
of first petal-fall,
announcement of death's commencement,
would take back
its flowering, claim glory.
So the rose and I
stood, terrified, at the beginning
of a new and beloved era.

It was pigeons, only pigeons
I'd startled from the porch rafters.
But the dread and hope
I carry with me
like lead and wings
let me believe otherwise.

True, none of this
has to do with heaven, since the sight
of those heavy birds flying away
reminded me
not so much of what's to come
as of what passes
away: birds,
hours, words, gestures, persons,
a drowned guitar in spring,
smell of lacquered wood
and wax when I prayed as a boy,
a pale cheek cut
by a green leaf,

the taste of blood
in a kiss,
someone whispering into someone's ear,
someone crying behind a door,
a clock dead at noon.
My father's hand
cupping my chin, weighing
tenderness between us,
pressing my mother's hip, weighing desire,
and cleaving a book open.
On the right of his hand, the words:
The Song of Songs, which is Solomon's.
Let him kiss me with the kisses of his mouth.
On the left of his hand the words:
For God shall bring every work
into judgement with every secret thing,
whether it be good,
or whether it be evil.
Outside his window, his rose,
aphid-eaten, bad-weather-wracked,
stem and thorn,
crook and bramble groping,
gripping brick, each sickly
bloom uttering, *I shall not die!*
before it's dispersed.

5.

My father wandered,
me beside him, human,
erect, unlike
roses. And, unlike
Paul, we had no mission,
though he loved Paul, read him continually
as, republic to republic,
oligarchy to anarchy to democracy, we arrived.

Once, while I walked
with my father, a man
reached out, touched his arm, said, *Kuo Yuan?*
The way he stared and spoke my father's name,
I thought he meant to ask, *Are you a dream?*
Here was the sadness of ten thousand miles,
of an abandoned house in Nan Jing,
where my father helped a blind man
wash his wife's newly dead body,
then bury it, while bombs
fell, and trees raised
charred arms and burned.
Here was a man who remembered
the sound of another's footfalls
so well as to call to him
after twenty years
on a sidewalk in America.

America, where, in Chicago, Little Chinatown,
who should I see
on the corner of Argyle and Broadway
but Li Bai and Du Fu, those two
poets of the wanderer's heart.

Folding paper boats,
they sent them swirling
down little rivers of gutter water.
Gold-toothed, cigarettes rolled in their sleeves,
they noted my dumb surprise:
What did you expect? Where else should we be?

6.

It goes on and it goes on,
the ceaseless invention, incessant
constructions and deconstructions
of shadows over black grass,
while, overhead, poplars
rock and nod,
wrestle *No* and *Yes*, contend
moon, no moon.
To think of the sea
is to hear in the sound of trees
the sound of the sea's work,
the wave's labor to change
the shore, not for the shore's sake, nor the wave's,
certainly not for me,
hundreds of miles from sea,
unless you count
my memory, my traverse
of sea one way to here.
I'm like my landlocked poplars: far
from water, I'm full of the sound of water.

But sea-sound differs from the sound of trees:
it owns a rhythm, almost
a meaning, but
no human story,
and so is like
the sound of trees,
tirelessly building
as wind builds, rising
as wind rises, steadily gathering
to nothing, quiet, and
the wind rising again.

The night grows
miscellaneous in the sound of trees.

But I own a human story,
whose very telling
remarks loss.
The characters survive through the telling,
the teller survives
by his telling; by his voice
brinking silence does he survive.
But, no one
can tell without cease
our human
story, and so we
lose, lose.

Yet, behind the sound
of trees is another
sound. Sometimes, lying
awake, or standing
like this in the yard, I hear it. It
ties our human telling
to its course
by momentum, and ours
is merely part
of its unbroken
stream, the human
and otherwise simultaneously
told. The past
doesn't fall away, the past
joins the greater
telling, and is.

At times its theme seems
murky, other times clear. Always,
death is a phrase, but just
a phrase, since nothing is ever
lost, and lives
are fulfilled by subsequence.
Listen, you can hear it: indescribable,
neither grief nor joy, neither mine nor yours....

But I'll not widow the world.
I'll tell my human
tale, tell it against
the current of that vaster, that
inhuman telling.
I'll measure time by losses and destructions.
Because the world
is so rich in detail, all of it so frail;
because all I love is imperfect;
because my memory's flaw
isn't in retention but organization;
because no one asked.

I'll tell once and for all
how someone lived.
Born on an island ruled by a petty soldier,
he was wrapped in bright cloth
and bound to his mother's hip,
where he rode until he could walk.
He did not utter a sound his first three years,
and his parents frowned.
Then, on the first night of their first exile,
he spoke out in complete sentences,
a Malaysian so lovely it was true song.

But when he spoke again
it was plain, artless, and twenty years later.
He wore a stranger's clothes,
he married a woman who tasted of iron and milk.
They had two sons, the namesakes
of a great emperor and a good-hearted bandit.
And always he stood erect to praise or grieve,
and knelt to live a while
at the level of his son's eyes.

7.

Tonight, someone, unable
to see in one darkness,
has shut his eyes
to see into another.
Among the sleepers, he is one
who doesn't sleep.
Know him by his noise.
Hear the nervous
scratching of his pencil,
sound of a rasping
file, a small
restless percussion, a soul's
minute chewing,
the old poem
birthing itself
into the new
and murderous century.

II

The Interrogation

Two streams: one dry, one poured all night by our beds.

I'll wonder
about neither.

The dry one was clogged with bodies.

I'm through
with memory.

At which window of what house did light teach you tedium?
On which step of whose stairway did you learn indecision?

I'm through
sorting avenues and doors,
curating houses and deaths.

Which house did we flee by night? Which house did we flee by day?

Don't ask me.

We stood and watched one burn; from one we ran away.

I'm neatly folding
the nights and days, notes
to be forgotten.

We were diminished. We were not spared. There was no pity.
Neither was their sanctuary. Neither rest.
There were fires in the streets. We stood among men, at the level
of their hands, all those wrists, dead or soon to die.

No more
letting my survival
depend on memory.

There was the sea; its green volume brought despair.
There was waiting, there was leaving. There was
astonishment too. The astonishment of
"I thought you died!" "How did you get out?"
"And Little Fei Fei walked right by the guards!"

I grow
leaden with stories,
my son's eyelids
grow heavy.

Who rowed the boat when our father tired?

Don't ask me.

Who came along? Who got left behind?

Ask the sea.

Through it all there was no song, and weeping
came many years later.

I'm through
with memory.

Sometimes a song,
even when there was weeping.

I'm through with memory.

Can't you still smell the smoke on my body?

✣

This Hour and What Is Dead

Tonight my brother, in heavy boots, is walking
through bare rooms over my head,
opening and closing doors.
What could he be looking for in an empty house?
What could he possibly need there in heaven?
Does he remember his earth, his birthplace set to torches?
His love for me feels like spilled water
running back to its vessel.

At this hour, what is dead is restless
and what is living is burning.

Someone tell him he should sleep now.

My father keeps a light on by our bed
and readies for our journey.
He mends ten holes in the knees
of five pairs of boy's pants.
His love for me is like his sewing:
various colors and too much thread,
the stitching uneven. But the needle pierces
clean through with each stroke of his hand.

At this hour, what is dead is worried
and what is living is fugitive.

Someone tell him he should sleep now.

God, that old furnace, keeps talking
with his mouth of teeth,
a beard stained at feasts, and his breath
of gasoline, airplane, human ash.
His love for me feels like fire,
feels like doves, feels like river-water.

At this hour, what is dead is helpless, kind
and helpless. While the Lord lives.

Someone tell the Lord to leave me alone.
I've had enough of his love
that feels like burning and flight and running away.

✣

Arise, Go Down

It wasn't the bright hems of the Lord's skirts
that brushed my face and I opened my eyes
to see from a cleft in rock His backside;

it's a wasp perched on my left cheek. I keep
my eyes closed and stand perfectly still
in the garden till it leaves me alone,

not to contemplate how this century
ends and the next begins with no one
I know having seen God, but to wonder

why I get through most days unscathed, though I
live in a time when it might be otherwise,
and I grow more fatherless each day.

For years now I have come to conclusions
without my father's help, discovering
on my own what I know, what I don't know,

and seeing how one cancels the other.
I've become a scholar of cancellations.
Here, I stand among my father's roses

and see that what punctures outnumbers what
consoles, the cruel and the tender never
make peace, though one climbs, though one descends

petal by petal to the hidden ground
no one owns. I see that which is taken
away by violence or persuasion.

The rose announces on earth the kingdom
of gravity. A bird cancels it.
My eyelids cancel the bird. Anything

might cancel my eyes: distance, time, war.
My father said, *Never take your both eyes*
off of the world, before he rocked me.

All night we waited for the knock
that would have signalled, *All clear, come now;*
it would have meant escape; it never came.

I didn't make the world I leave you with,
he said, and then, being poor, he left me
only this world, in which there is always

a family waiting in terror
before they're rended, this world wherein a man
might arise, go down, and walk along a path

and pause and bow to roses, roses
his father raised, and admire them, for one moment
unable, thank God, to see in each and
every flower the world cancelling itself.

My Father, in Heaven, Is Reading Out Loud

My father, in heaven, is reading out loud
to himself Psalms or news. Now he ponders what
he's read. No. He is listening for the sound
of children in the yard. Was that laughing
or crying? So much depends upon the
answer, for either he will go on reading,
or he'll run to save a child's day from grief.
As it is in heaven, so it was on earth.

Because my father walked the earth with a grave,
determined rhythm, my shoulders ached
from his gaze. Because my father's shoulders
ached from the pulling of oars, my life now moves
with a powerful back-and-forth rhythm:
nostalgia, speculation. Because he
made me recite a book a month, I forget
everything as soon as I read it. And knowledge
never comes but while I'm mid-stride a flight
of stairs, or lost a moment on some avenue.

A remarkable disappointment to him,
I am like anyone who arrives late
in the millennium and is unable
to stay to the end of days. The world's
beginnings are obscure to me, its outcomes
inaccessible. I don't understand
the source of starlight, or starlight's destinations.
And already another year slides out

of balance. But I don't disparage scholars;
my father was one and I loved him,
who packed his books once, and all of our belongings,
then sat down to await instruction
from his god, yes, but also from a radio.
At the doorway, I watched, and I suddenly
knew he was one like me, who got my learning
under a lintel; he was one of the powerless,
to whom knowledge came while he sat among
suitcases, boxes, old newspapers, string.

He did not decide peace or war, home or exile,
escape by land or escape by sea.
He waited merely, as always someone
waits, far, near, here, hereafter, to find out:
is it praise or lament hidden in the next moment?

✥

For a New Citizen of These United States

Forgive me for thinking I saw
the irregular postage stamp of death;
a black moth the size of my left
thumbnail is all I've trapped in the damask.
There is no need for alarm. And

there is no need for sadness, if
the rain at the window now reminds you
of nothing; not even of that
parlor, long like a nave, where cloud-shadow,
wing-shadow, where father-shadow
continually confused the light. In flight,
leaf-throng and, later, soldiers and
flags deepened those windows to submarine.

But you don't remember, I know,
so I won't mention that house where Chung hid,
Lin wizened, you languished, and Ming—
Ming hush-hushed us with small song. And since you
don't recall the missionary
bells chiming the hour, or those words whose sounds
alone exhaust the heart—*garden,*
heaven, amen—I'll mention none of it.

After all, it was just our life,
merely years in a book of years. It was
1960, and we stood with
the other families on a crowded
railroad platform. The trains came, then
the rains, and then we got separated.

And in the interval between
familiar faces, events occurred, which
one of us faithfully pencilled
in a day-book bound by a rubber band.

But birds, as you say, fly forward.
So I won't show you letters and the shawl
I've so meaninglessly preserved.
And I won't hum along, if you don't, when
our mothers sing *Nights in Shanghai.*
I won't, each Spring, each time I smell lilac,
recall my mother, patiently
stitching money inside my coat lining,
if you don't remember your mother
preparing for your own escape.

After all, it was only our
life, our life and its forgetting.

With Ruins

Choose a quiet
place, a ruins, a house no more
a house,
under whose stone archway I stood
one day to duck the rain.

The roofless floor, vertical
studs, eight wood columns
supporting nothing,
two staircases careening to nowhere, all
make it seem

a sketch, notes to a house, a three-
dimensional grid negotiating
absences,
an idea
receding into indefinite rain,

or else that idea
emerging, skeletal
against the hammered sky, a
human thing, scoured, seen clean
through from here to an iron heaven.

A place where things
were said and done,
there you can remember
what you need to
remember. Melancholy is useful. Bring yours.

There are no neighbors to wonder
who you are,
what you might be doing
walking there,
stopping now and then

to touch a crumbling brick
or stand in a doorway
framed by the day.
No one has to know you
think of another doorway

that framed the rain or news of war
depending on which way you faced.
You think of sea-roads and earth-roads
you traveled once, and always
in the same direction: away.

You think
of a woman, a favorite
dress, your old father's breasts
the last time you saw him, his breath,
brief, the leaf

you've torn from a vine and which you hold now
to your cheek like a train ticket
or a piece of cloth, a little hand or a blade—
it all depends
on the course of your memory.

It's a place
for those who own no place
to correspond to ruins in the soul.
It's mine.
It's all yours.

❖

III

This Room and Everything in It

Lie still now
while I prepare for my future,
certain hard days ahead,
when I'll need what I know so clearly this moment.

I am making use
of the one thing I learned
of all the things my father tried to teach me:
the art of memory.

I am letting this room
and everything in it
stand for my ideas about love
and its difficulties.

I'll let your love-cries,
those spacious notes
of a moment ago,
stand for distance.

Your scent,
that scent
of spice and a wound,
I'll let stand for mystery.

Your sunken belly
is the daily cup
of milk I drank
as a boy before morning prayer.

The sun on the face
of the wall
is God, the face
I can't see, my soul,

and so on, each thing
standing for a separate idea,
and those ideas forming the constellation
of my greater idea.
And one day, when I need
to tell myself something intelligent
about love,

I'll close my eyes
and recall this room and everything in it:
My body is estrangement.
This desire, perfection.
Your closed eyes my extinction.
Now I've forgotten my
idea. The book
on the windowsill, riffled by wind . . .
the even-numbered pages are
the past, the odd-
numbered pages, the future.
The sun is
God, your body is milk . . .

useless, useless . . .
your cries are song, my body's not me . . .
no good . . . my idea
has evaporated . . . your hair is time, your thighs are song . . .
it had something to do
with death . . . it had something
to do with love.

❖

The City in Which I Love You

I will arise now, and go
about the city in the streets,
and in the broad ways I will seek. . .
whom my soul loveth.
SONG OF SONGS 3:2

And when, in the city in which I love you,
even my most excellent song goes unanswered,
and I mount the scabbed streets,
the long shouts of avenues,
and tunnel sunken night in search of you....

That I negotiate fog, bituminous
rain ringing like teeth into the beggar's tin,
or two men jackaling a third in some alley
weirdly lit by a couch on fire, that I
drag my extinction in search of you....

Past the guarded schoolyards, the boarded-up churches, swastikaed
synagogues, defended houses of worship, past
newspapered windows of tenements, among the violated,
the prosecuted citizenry, throughout this
storied, buttressed, scavenged, policed
city I call home, in which I am a guest....

A bruise, blue
in the muscle, you
impinge upon me.
As bone hugs the ache home, so
I'm vexed to love you, your body

the shape of returns, your hair a torso
of light, your heat
I must have, your opening
I'd eat, each moment
of that soft-finned fruit,
inverted fountain in which I don't see me.

My tongue remembers your wounded flavor.
The vein in my neck
adores you. A sword
stands up between my hips,
my hidden fleece sends forth its scent of human oil.

The shadows under my arms,
I promise, are tender, the shadows
under my face. Do not calculate,
but come, smooth other, rough sister.
Yet, how will you know me

among the captives, my hair grown long,
my blood motley, my ways trespassed upon?
In the uproar, the confusion
of accents and inflections,
how will you hear me when I open my mouth?

Look for me, one of the drab population
under fissured edifices, fractured
artifices. Make my various
names flock overhead,
I will follow you.
Hew me to your beauty.

Stack in me the unaccountable fire,
bring on me the iron leaf, but tenderly.
Folded one hundred times and
creased, I'll not crack.
Threshed to excellence, I'll achieve you.

But in the city
in which I love you,
no one comes, no one
meets me in the brick clefts;
in the wedged dark,

no finger touches me secretly, no mouth
tastes my flawless salt,
no one wakens the honey in the cells, finds the humming
in the ribs, the rich business in the recesses;
hulls clogged, I continue laden, translated

by exhaustion and time's appetite, my sleep abandoned
in bus stations and storefront stoops,
my insomnia erected under a sky
cross-hatched by wires, branches,
and black flights of rain. Lewd body of wind

jams me in the passageways, doors slam
like guns going off, a gun goes off, a pie plate spins
past, whizzing its thin tremolo,
a plastic bag, fat with wind, barrels by and slaps
a chain-link fence, wraps it like clung skin.

In the excavated places,
I waited for you, and I did not cry out.
In the derelict rooms, my body needed you,
and there was such flight in my breast.
During the daily assaults, I called to you,

and my voice pursued you,
even backward
to that other city
in which I saw a woman
squat in the street

beside a body,
and fan with a handkerchief flies from its face.
That woman
was not me. And
the corpse

lying there, lying there
so still it seemed with great effort, as though
his whole being was concentrating on the hole
in his forehead, so still
I expected he'd sit up any minute and laugh out loud:

that man was not me;
his wound was his, his death not mine.
And the soldier
who fired the shot, then lit a cigarette:
he was not me.

And the ones I do not see
in cities all over the world,
the ones sitting, standing, lying down, those
in prisons playing checkers with their knocked-out teeth:
they are not me. Some of them are

my age, even my height and weight;
none of them is me.
The woman who is slapped, the man who is kicked,
the ones who don't survive,
whose names I do not know;

they are not me forever,
the ones who no longer live
in the cities in which
you are not,
the cities in which I looked for you.

The rain stops, the moon
in her breaths appears overhead.
The only sound now is a far flapping.
Over the National Bank, the flag of some republic or other
gallops like water or fire to tear itself away.

If I feel the night
move to disclosures or crescendos,
it's only because I'm famished
for meaning; the night
merely dissolves.

And your otherness is perfect as my death.
Your otherness exhausts me,
like looking suddenly up from here
to impossible stars fading.
Everything is punished by your absence.

Is prayer, then, the proper attitude
for the mind that longs to be freely blown,
but which gets snagged on the barb
called *world*, that
tooth-ache, the actual? What prayer

would I build? And to whom?
Where are you
in the cities in which I love you,
the cities daily risen to work and to money,
to the magnificent miles and the gold coasts?

Morning comes to this city vacant of you.
Pages and windows flare, and you are not there.
Someone sweeps his portion of sidewalk,
wakens the drunk, slumped like laundry,
and you are gone.

You are not in the wind
which someone notes in the margins of a book.
You are gone out of the small fires in abandoned lots
where human figures huddle,
each aspiring to its own ghost.

Between brick walls, in a space no wider than my face,
a leafless sapling stands in mud.
In its branches, a nest of raw mouths
gaping and cheeping, scrawny fires that must eat.
My hunger for you is no less than theirs.

At the gates of the city in which I love you,
the sea hauls the sun on its back,
strikes the land, which rebukes it.
What ardor in its sliding heft,
a flameless friction on the rocks.

Like the sea, I am recommended by my orphaning.
Noisy with telegrams not received,
quarrelsome with aliases,
intricate with misguided journeys,
by my expulsions have I come to love you.

Straight from my father's wrath,
and long from my mother's womb,
late in this century and on a Wednesday morning,
bearing the mark of one who's experienced
neither heaven nor hell,

my birthplace vanished, my citizenship earned,
in league with stones of the earth, I
enter, without retreat or help from history,
the days of no day, my earth
of no earth, I re-enter

the city in which I love you.
And I never believed that the multitude
of dreams and many words were vain.

IV

The Waiting

Now between your eyes
the furrows shine,
while your flushed
oval face floats
above the steaming
bath water.
Your shoulders roll, hips
sway side
to side,
legs stretch, rub together;
you call this luxury;
you pant a little;
your eyes close beneath
a thought. What, I wonder. Tonight
I'm saddened by those two
lines on your forehead,
by the knowledge
that each of their twins
lies here, between my own
eyes. Years
ago a man
and woman
quarrel,
waken their son. The woman runs
into the bedroom the three share and soothes him, while
in the other
room waits the man, who, if
he hears any
of what's going on
in the city—
traffic, the neighbor's TV, music
from an upstairs balcony,

his wife lilting
a child's tune—if he hears,
doesn't give it
away, this man
who one day
woke to find his life
hard, and who now
waits standing, too eager
to sit, the apartment too
small to pace, standing,
not to be caught
sitting in a life
toward which he came by device
and bad luck.
Her song ends, but she won't come, so he goes
in, to find
woman and child
asleep on the bed.
He lifts the small body
and lays him in his little bed by the wall.
He lies down by his wife.

I don't remember if he lay there remembering—
I hope he did, it
would have helped—
how they two, one year back, after hours
of rocking the child, an infant then,
began to make love,
and how the boy
wakened crying.
I hope
he closed his eyes to see
how the woman, naked, rose
to bring the baby to their bed, and, lying

with her back to the man,
suckled the boy while
the man lay longing, hard yet, thighs wet
from her, and on his chest
her odor.

By murmurs and thingless words
the mother answers
her son's sucking, his
gulping and mewling.
Rolling towards them, the man
reaches around her waist to stroke the boy's head.
Slowly, she reaches behind
and clasps him, fastens
him to her, while he
half mounts her damp length,
and spills his semen between her knees.
Exhausted, the three
bodies, complicated
thus, sleep a few hours,
until one rises
for work, in light
the color of breast milk drained on the sheet.

Love, these lines
accompany our want, nameless
or otherwise, and our waiting.
And since we've not learned
how not to want,
we've had to learn,
by waiting, how to wait.
So I wait
well, while you bathe.
Feet apart, you squat; shoulders stooped, you reach
beneath to wash, and then I see

the mole on your right side, under your arm,
and I know—such knowledge
beautiful in its uselessness—
that it lies from your nipple
a distance precisely measured
by my left hand,
forefinger to wrist.
Now your legs fold
under, big slabs of water
slide up the tub
then down to clap
your hips and belly.
You sit atop your legs to wash your belly,
loose, soft from lately
birthing again, and streaked
with running milk, that pale fluid,
sweet, iron, astonishingly thin.

A Story

Sad is the man who is asked for a story
and can't come up with one.

His five-year-old son waits in his lap.
Not the same story, Baba. A new one.
The man rubs his chin, scratches his ear.

In a room full of books in a world
of stories, he can recall
not one, and soon, he thinks, the boy
will give up on his father.

Already the man lives far ahead, he sees
the day this boy will go. *Don't go!*
Hear the alligator story! The angel story once more!
You love the spider story. You laugh at the spider.
Let me tell it!

But the boy is packing his shirts,
he is looking for his keys. *Are you a god,*
the man screams, *that I sit mute before you?*
Am I a god that I should never disappoint?

But the boy is here. *Please, Baba, a story?*
It is an emotional rather than logical equation,
an earthly rather than heavenly one,
which posits that a boy's supplications
and a father's love add up to silence.

Goodnight

You've stopped whispering
and are asleep. I go on listening

to apples drop in the grass
beyond the window. Earlier we tried to guess

each fall's moment, but neither kept up
that little game of hope

or fear for long. Now, your weight
against me is like . . . I was about to say

like no other, unmistakably
human, my son's. But, truth is, you're simply

heft. Burden like, say, grain,
your body brings my body pain,

your shoulders, knees, elbows, hands,
lumpy like sacked fruit, and

whatever concord is
actual between us is

not easily meant,
but is so only by our diligence.

I recall a far
season of flowers

when, for love, I crept to the edge of a roof to reach
a petal-decked branch.

It snapped, I
dropped, screaming down sky

and flowering. My father yelled
my name, ran out to find me sprawled,

dazed, gripping his crushed gift, thrust
at him in my bloody fist.

He plunges below us now, as we
fall soundless toward him, our bodies

crowded on your narrow bed,
my arm and leg gone numb, your torso wedged

between the wall and me.
You sleep uncomfortably,

though comforted by my
presence, for which you cry

some nights, and which you, such nights, endure.
Where did you, so young, learn

such sacrifice? Now
I no longer hear the apples fall. But how

they go! Incessantly, though
with no noise, no

blunt announcements of their gravity.
See!

There is no bottom to the night, no end
to our descent.

We suffer each other to have each other a while.

You Must Sing

He sings in his father's arms, sings his father
to sleep, all the while seeing how on that face
grown suddenly strange, wasting to shadow,
time moves. Stern time. Sweet time. Because his father

asked, he sings; because they are wholly lost.
How else, in immaculate noon, will each find
each, who are so close now? So close and lost.
His voice stands at windows, runs everywhere.

Was death giant? O, how will he find his
father? They are so close. Was death a guest?
By which door did it come? All the day's doors
are closed. He must go out of those hours, that house,

the enfolding limbs, go burdened to learn:
you must sing to be found; when found, you must sing.

Here I Am

I wait. I don't go. He will come, the one
who waited for me each day
at the edge of the schoolyard.

I wait. And I am bitten thin
by waiting. And I grow
dense with luggage and time.

He will come, though
he may never come, who wrote his name
by drawing a spear borne in a heart.

In this life, this is how
one must wait, past despair,
the heart a fossil, the minutes molten, the feet turned to stone.

I know a boy who fell asleep
one second before his father returned, his name
a lozenge thinning on his father's tongue.

I've heard of prisoners who died
a minute before rescue.
Such waiting has nothing to do with hope;

it has less to do with patience;
it's simply the way a soul is bent.
Such waiting is impossible.

But I wait,
for it's the only
possibility left to me.

And though I stopped waiting years ago,
I continue to wait.
Even now

he comes, whom death has made giant.
And small as the rain
and as many.

Whose Sabbath shoes
I blackened each Saturday
and buffed to hard armor.

Who set me on a chair and two dictionaries
and made me read an old book
of ancient and terrifying stories

while sucking butterscotch drops
he unwrapped for me.
Sweet learning, he called it.

Even now,
no one comes,
though I sense his pure approach.

Maybe he is lost,
the lonely one
who is no longer lonely.

Maybe he waits for me.
Maybe he fears he is forgotten,
the way I am forgotten,

each of us the one
who, in that childhood game, shouts,
though no one hears, *Here I am!*

A Final Thing

I am that last, that
final thing, the body
in a white sheet listening,

the whole of me trained,
curled like one great ear on
a sound, a noise I know, a

woman talking
in another room,
the woman I love; and

though I can't hear
her words, by their voicing
I can guess

she is telling a story,

using a voice which speaks to another,
weighted with that other's attention,
and avowing it
by deepening in intention.

Rich with the fullness of what's declared,
this voice points
away from itself
to some place

in the hearer,
sends the hearer back
to himself
to find what he knows.

A saying full of hearing,
a murmuring full of telling
and compassion for the listener
and for what's told,

now interrupted by a second voice,

thinner, higher, uncertain.
Querying, it seems
an invitation to be met,
stirring anticipation, embodying
incompletion of time and the day.

My son, my first-born, and his mother
are involved in a story no longer only theirs,
for I am implicated,
all three of us now
clinging to expectancy, riding sound and air.

Will my first morning of heaven be this?
No. And this is not
my last morning on earth.
I am simply last
in my house

to waken, and the first
sound I hear
is the voice of one I love
speaking to one we love.
I hear it through the bedroom wall;

something, someday, I'll close my eyes to recall.

V

The Cleaving

He gossips like my grandmother, this man
with my face, and I could stand
amused all afternoon
in the Hon Kee Grocery,
amid hanging meats he
chops: roast pork cut
from a hog hung
by nose and shoulders,
her entire skin burnt
crisp, flesh I know
to be sweet,
her shining
face grinning
up at ducks
dangling single file,
each pierced by black
hooks through breast, bill,
and steaming from a hole
stitched shut at the ass.
I step to the counter, recite,
and he, without even slightly
varying the rhythm of his current confession or harangue,
scribbles my order on a greasy receipt,
and chops it up quick.

Such a sorrowful Chinese face,
nomad, Gobi, Northern
in its boniness
clear from the high
warlike forehead

to the sheer edge of the jaw.
He could be my brother, but finer,
and, except for his left forearm, which is engorged,
sinewy from his daily grip and
wield of a two-pound tool,
he's delicate, narrow-
waisted, his frame
so slight a lover, some
rough other
might break it down
its smooth, oily length.
In his light-handed calligraphy
on receipts and in his
moodiness, he is
a Southerner from a river-province;
suited for scholarship, his face poised
above an open book, he'd mumble
his favorite passages.
He could be my grandfather;
come to America to get a Western education
in 1917, but too homesick to study,
he sits in the park all day, reading poems
and writing letters to his mother.

He lops the head off, chops
the neck of the duck
into six, slits
the body
open, groin
to breast, and drains
the scalding juices,
then quarters the carcass
with two fast hacks of the cleaver,
old blade that has worn
into the surface of the round

foot-thick chop-block
a scoop that cradles precisely the curved steel.

The head, flung from the body, opens
down the middle where the butcher
cleanly halved it between
the eyes, and I
see, foetal-crouched
inside the skull, the homunculus,
gray brain grainy
to eat.
Did this animal, after all, at the moment
its neck broke,
image the way his executioner
shrinks from his own death?
Is this how
I, too, recoil from my day?
See how this shape
hordes itself, see how
little it is.
See its grease on the blade.
Is this how I'll be found
when judgement is passed, when names
are called, when crimes are tallied?
This is also how I looked before I tore my mother open.
Is this how I presided over my century, is this how
I regarded the murders?
This is also how I prayed.
Was it me in the Other
I prayed to when I prayed?
This too was how I slept, clutching my wife.
Was it me in the other I loved
when I loved another?
The butcher sees me eye this delicacy.
With a finger, he picks it

out of the skull-cradle
and offers it to me.
I take it gingerly between my fingers
and suck it down.
I eat my man.

The noise the body makes
when the body meets
the soul over the soul's ocean and penumbra
is the old sound of up-and-down, in-and-out,
a lump of muscle chug-chugging blood
into the ear; a lover's
heart-shaped tongue;
flesh rocking flesh until flesh comes;
the butcher working
at his block and blade to marry their shapes
by violence and time;
an engine crossing,
re-crossing salt water, hauling
immigrants and the junk
of the poor. These
are the faces I love, the bodies
and scents of bodies
for which I long
in various ways, at various times,
thirteen gathered around the redwood,
happy, talkative, voracious
at day's end,
eager to eat
four kinds of meat
prepared four different ways,
numerous plates and bowls of rice and vegetables,
each made by distinct affections
and brought to table by many hands.

Brothers and sisters by blood and design,
who sit in separate bodies of varied shapes,
we constitute a many-membered
body of love.
In a world of shapes
of my desires, each one here
is a shape of one of my desires, and each
is known to me and dear by virtue
of each one's unique corruption
of those texts, the face, the body:
that jut jaw
to gnash tendon;
that wide nose to meet the blows
a face like that invites;
those long eyes closing on the seen;
those thick lips
to suck the meat of animals
or recite 300 poems of the T'ang;
these teeth to bite my monosyllables;
these cheekbones to make
those syllables sing the soul.
Puffed or sunken
according to the life,
dark or light according
to the birth, straight
or humped, whole, manqué, quasi, each pleases, verging
on utter grotesquery.
All are beautiful by variety.
The soul too
is a debasement
of a text, but, thus, it
acquires salience, although a
human salience, but
inimitable, and, hence, memorable.
God is the text.

The soul is a corruption
and a mnemonic.

A bright moment,
I hold up an old head
from the sea and admire the haughty
down-curved mouth
that seems to disdain
all the eyes are blind to,
including me, the eater.
Whole unto itself, complete
without me, yet its
shape complements the shape of my mind.
I take it as text and evidence
of the world's love for me,
and I feel urged to utterance,
urged to read the body of the world, urged
to say it
in human terms,
my reading a kind of eating, my eating
a kind of reading,
my saying a diminishment, my noise
a love-in-answer.
What is it in me would
devour the world to utter it?
What is it in me will not let
the world be, would eat
not just this fish,
but the one who killed it,
the butcher who cleaned it.
I would eat the way he
squats, the way he
reaches into the plastic tubs
and pulls out a fish, clubs it, takes it
to the sink, guts it, drops it on the weighing pan.

I would eat that thrash
and plunge of the watery body
in the water, that liquid violence
between the man's hands,
I would eat
the gutless twitching on the scales,
three pounds of dumb
nerve and pulse, I would eat it all
to utter it.
The deaths at the sinks, those bodies prepared
for eating, I would eat,
and the standing deaths
at the counters, in the aisles,
the walking deaths in the streets,
the death-far-from-home, the death-
in-a-strange-land, these Chinatown
deaths, these American deaths.
I would devour this race to sing it,
this race that according to Emerson
managed to preserve to a hair
for three or four thousand years
the ugliest features in the world.
I would eat these features, eat
the last three or four thousand years, every hair.
And I would eat Emerson, his transparent soul, his
soporific transcendence.
I would eat this head,
glazed in pepper-speckled sauce,
the cooked eyes opaque in their sockets.
I bring it to my mouth and—
the way I was taught, the way I've watched
others before me do—
with a stiff tongue lick out
the cheek-meat and the meat
over the armored jaw, my eating,

its sensual, salient nowness,
punctuating the void
from which such hunger springs and to which it proceeds.

And what
is this
I excavate
with my mouth?
What is this
plated, ribbed, hinged
architecture, this *carp head*,
but one more
articulation of a single nothing
severally manifested?
What is my eating,
rapt as it is,
but another
shape of going,
my immaculate expiration?

O, nothing is so
steadfast it won't go
the way the body goes.
The body goes.
The body's grave,
so serious
in its dying,
arduous as martyrs
in that task and as
glorious. It goes
empty always
and announces its going
by spasms and groans, farts and sweats.

What I thought were the arms
aching *cleave*, were the knees trembling *leave*.
What I thought were the muscles
insisting *resist, persist, exist,*
were the pores
hissing *mist* and *waste*.
What I thought was the body humming *reside, reside,*
was the body sighing *revise, revise*.
O, the murderous deletions, the keening
down to nothing, the cleaving.
All of the body's revisions end
in death.
All of the body's revisions end.

Bodies eating bodies, heads eating heads,
we are nothing eating nothing,
and though we feast,
are filled, overfilled,
we go famished.
We gang the doors of death.
That is, our deaths are fed
that we may continue our daily dying,
our bodies going
down, while the plates-soon-empty
are passed around, that true
direction of our true prayers,
while the butcher spells
his message, manifold,
in the mortal air.
He coaxes, cleaves, brings change
before our very eyes, and at every
moment of our being.
As we eat we're eaten.

Else what is this
violence, this salt, this
passion, this heaven?

I thought the soul an airy thing.
I did not know the soul
is cleaved so that the soul might be restored.
Live wood hewn,
its sap springs from a sticky wound.
No seed, no egg has he
whose business calls for an axe.
In the trade of my soul's shaping,
he traffics in hews and hacks.

No easy thing, violence.
One of its names? Change. Change
resides in the embrace
of the effaced and the effacer,
in the covenant of the opened and the opener;
the axe accomplishes it on the soul's axis.
What then may I do
but cleave to what cleaves me.
I kiss the blade and eat my meat.
I thank the wielder and receive,
while terror spirits
my change, sorrow also.
The terror the butcher
scripts in the unhealed
air, the sorrow of his Shang
dynasty face,
African face with slit eyes. He is
my sister, this
beautiful Bedouin, this Shulamite,
keeper of sabbaths, diviner

of holy texts, this dark
dancer, this Jew, this Asian, this one
with the Cambodian face, Vietnamese face, this Chinese
I daily face,
this immigrant,
this man with my own face.

Acknowledgments

I am indebted to the Illinois Arts Council, the National Endowment for the Arts, the Mrs. Giles Whiting Foundation and the John Simon Guggenheim Memorial Foundation for grants which greatly aided in the completion of this book.

—L-Y. L.

Grateful acknowledgment is made to the editors of the following journals in which some of these poems (or earlier versions of them) originally appeared:

The American Poetry Review: "This Room and Everything in It"

The American Voice: "A Story"

Grand Street: "My Father, in Heaven, Is Reading Out Loud," "The Interrogation" and "The City in Which I Love You"

Ironwood: "Furious Versions"

Ploughshares: "This Hour and What Is Dead"

TriQuarterly: "The Cleaving" and "The Waiting"

"Furious Versions" was also collected in *The Pushcart Prize XIII.*

Li-Young Lee

Li-Young Lee was born in 1957 in Jakarta, Indonesia, of Chinese parents. In 1959, his father, after spending a year as a political prisoner in President Sukarno's jails, fled Indonesia with his family. Between 1959 and 1964 they traveled in Hong Kong, Macau, and Japan, until arriving in America.

Mr. Lee has studied at the University of Pittsburgh, the University of Arizona, and the State University of New York, College at Brockport. He has taught at various universities, including Northwestern University and the University of Iowa. In 1990 Li-Young Lee traveled in China and Indonesia to do personal research for a book of autobiographical prose.

Li-Young Lee's several honors include grants from the Illinois Arts Council, The Commonwealth of Pennsylvania, the Pennsylvania Council on the Arts, and the National Endowment for the Arts. In 1989 he was awarded a fellowship by the John Simon Guggenheim Memorial Foundation; in 1988 he was the recipient of a Writer's Award from the Mrs. Giles Whiting Foundation. In 1987 Mr. Lee received New York University's Delmore Schwartz Memorial Poetry Award for his first book, *Rose,* published by BOA Editions, Ltd. in 1986; and *The City in Which I Love You,* Li-Young Lee's second book of poems, was the 1990 Lamont Poetry Selection of The Academy of American Poets.

Li-Young Lee currently resides in Chicago, Illinois, with his wife, Donna, and their children.

BOA Editions. Ltd.
American Poets Continuum Series

Vol. 1 *The Führer Bunker: A Cycle of Poems in Progress*
W. D. Snodgrass
Vol. 2 *She*
M. L. Rosenthal
Vol. 3 *Living with Distance*
Ralph J. Mills, Jr.
Vol. 4 *Not Just Any Death*
Michael Waters
Vol. 5 *That Was Then: New and Selected Poems*
Isabella Gardner
Vol. 6 *Things That Happen Where There Aren't Any People*
William Stafford
Vol. 7 *The Bridge of Change: Poems 1974-1980*
John Logan
Vol. 8 *Signatures*
Joseph Stroud
Vol. 9 *People Live Here: Selected Poems 1949-1983*
Louis Simpson
Vol. 10 *Yin*
Carolyn Kizer
Vol. 11 *Duhamel: Ideas of Order in Little Canada*
Bill Tremblay
Vol. 12 *Seeing It Was So*
Anthony Piccione
Vol. 13 *Hyam Plutzik: The Collected Poems*
Vol. 14 *Good Woman: Poems and a Memoir 1965-1980*
Lucille Clifton
Vol. 15 *Next: New Poems*
Lucille Clifton
Vol. 16 *Roxa: Voices of the Culver Family*
William B. Patrick
Vol. 17 *John Logan: The Collected Poems*
Vol. 18 *Isabella Gardner: The Collected Poems*
Vol. 19 *The Sunken Lightship*
Peter Makuck
Vol. 20 *The City in Which I Love You*
Li-Young Lee

feeling that can't understand
poetry + politics —

Address weaknesses
— broad range of course

[illegible] to make it meaningful.